DOGS
DOGS
DOGS

DOGS DOGS DOGS

A COLLECTION OF
GREAT DOG CARTOONS
EDITED BY S. GROSS

HARPER & ROW, PUBLISHERS, New York
Cambridge, Philadelphia, San Francisco, London
Mexico City, São Paulo, Singapore, Sydney

Some of the cartoons in this collection have appeared in the following periodicals and are reprinted by permission of the authors: *American Health, Audubon, Boston Phoenix, Chicago Magazine, Christian Science Monitor, Diversion, Fantasy and Science Fiction, Good Housekeeping, Household, Ladies' Home Journal, In the Know, Look, National Lampoon, The New York Times, Psychology Today, Saturday Evening Post, Saturday Review, Scouting, This Week, Trial Diplomacy Journal, Wilson Library Bulletin, Woman's World.*

Grateful acknowledgment is made for permission to reprint:

The cartoon by Sergio Aragones on page 151 from *Mad Menagerie*. Copyright © 1983 by Sergio Aragones. Reprinted by permission of the author.

The cartoon by Mort Gerberg on page 96 from *Right On, Sister*. Copyright © 1971 by Mort Gerberg. Reprinted by permission of the author.

The cartoon by Lo Linkert on page 56 from *Golf Digest*. Copyright © 1985 by Golf Digest/Tennis, Inc. Reprinted by permission of the author and *Golf Digest*.

The cartoon by Joseph Mirachi on page 10 from *Sports Illustrated*. Copyright © 1956 Time Inc.

The cartoon by Donald Orehek on page 119 from *50 Plus*. Reprinted by permission of *50 Plus* magazine. © Retirement Living Publishing Co., Inc.

The cartoon by Brian Savage on page 62 from *OMNI*. Copyright © 1981 by Omni International Limited. Reprinted courtesy of *OMNI* magazine.

Cartoons copyrighted by *The New Yorker* are indicated throughout the book.

FIRST EDITION

Designer: Francesca Belanger

Library of Congress Cataloging in Publication Data
Main entry under title:

Dogs dogs dogs.

Includes index.
1. Dogs—Caricatures and cartoons. 2. American wit and humor, Pictorial. I. Gross, S. (Sam)
NC1426.D64 1985   741.5'973   85–42566
ISBN 0–06–015464–0

85 86 87 88 89 MPC 10 9 8 7 6 5 4 3 2 1

DOGS
DOGS
DOGS

"And *this,* I presume, is Fluffy?"

"Of course he said 'Arf.' What did you expect
his first word to be?" WILLIAM MAUL

ED FISHER

"It's for you."

"Tough work, owning a dog."

LIZA DONNELLY

"Well, I can see there *are* differences to work out, but basically,
I feel, you still have a sound dog-and-little-old-lady relationship."

JARED LEE

"Oh, Elizabeth! I didn't recognize you."

ED FRASCINO

"You really *are* man's best friend."

JERRY MARCUS

"Your exact words, as I recall, were: 'Her puppies
will sell like hotcakes!'"

DONALD OREHEK

BERNARD SCHOENBAUM

"He eats from the garbage, he could sleep in the garage,
and his wine only costs 98 cents a bottle.
Oh please, daddy, please can we keep him?"

TIM HAGGERTY

"I hope we're not intruding, but Chester picked up a trail
he couldn't let go of."

PETER STEINER

LEO CULLUM

"Maybe it's the propylene glycol you don't go for."

JOE MIRACHI

"Next!"

VAHAN SHIRVANIAN

"Unfortunately, I took him into one of those 'if you break it you bought it' places."

ANDY WYATT

BILL WOODMAN

ED FISHER

"OK, Binkie. You can let go of the slippers now."

PETER VEY

"Miss Olmstead, may we have another doggie treat?"

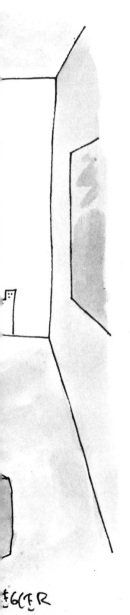

GOOD BOY!

WILLIAM MAUL

JACK ZIEGLER

15

BILL WOODMAN

16

"Why, no, I didn't see any fox go past here."

"Before we begin the board meeting, which one of you is going
to take this one last puppy off my hands?"

PETER STEINER

"We don't look much alike, but have you noticed that
our personalities are identical?"

ED FRASCINO

18

MORT GERBERG

CATHARINE O'NEILL

"Oh, it's quite all right to discuss him by name; Timmy's the kind of dog
who doesn't mind being referred to in the third person."

MORT GERBERG

"He's just warming it up for me."

ORLANDO BUSINO

NURIT KARLIN

TIM HAGGERTY

"On TV they run over to it and wag their tails."   SIDNEY HARRIS

"After ten years you're allowed to have a pet."

JOHN CALDWELL

"Next time just bring the slippers. I'll get the pipe myself!"

AARON BACALL

"I don't take you out enough."

BORIS DRUCKER

VAHAN SHIRVANIAN

"Sweetheart, could you maybe include the dog?"

BERNARD SCHOENBAUM

"Inflation, baby."

CHARLES SAUERS

"See? It's not as if you were the only one."

GAHAN WILSON

He's part shepherd...

'SIPRESS
DAVID SIPRESS

"What did you say to him?"

ED FRASCINO

"They all want doggie bags!"

JERRY MARCUS

"Now play dead."

"There's a reply to your ad for a companion."

DONALD OREHEK

FRANK MODELL

"Due to the sudden illness of one of our stars, the role of Clancy
will be essayed by yours truly."

BRIAN SAVAGE

A MAN AND
HIS DOG

CHARLES BARSOTTI
© 1980 The New Yorker Magazine, Inc.

"From the left: Jeremiah Brisco III, Anthony Cortland
of Sutherland Haven, Terhune Hempstead of Intervale-Hempstead,
Sir Fairmont Starspray of Griscombshire, Ferguson Fentlow
of Fairlea, and, of course, Al."

"Is wittle Pookah hungwy?"

JACK ZIEGLER

"I taught him to talk. . . . You teach him to shut up."

ANDY WYATT

34

MIKE TWOHY

"A kiss will break the enchantment and people will call me Prince again."

"Thanks."

ORLANDO BUSINO

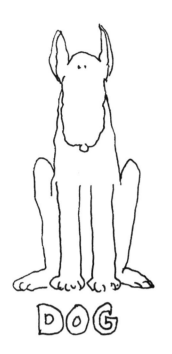

DOG DOGGIE DAWG

THOMAS CHENEY

"You mustn't wake him, Charles. He's walking in his sleep."

M. K. BROWN

37

1.

2.

3.

4.

5.

6. ▶

7.

8.

9.

WOODMAN

"No, no, Sparky. Stay!"

BUD GRACE

"I suppose you know you're spoiling that dog."

"I'm getting worried, doc—he's been playing dead
for two weeks now."

RICHARD ORLIN

"Hey, down in front!"

ARNIE LEVIN

CALLAHAN

JOHN CALLAHAN

"Just how big does he get?"

DONALD OREHEK

"Wellington is much improved with the loving care of those
three great physicians, *nature, time,* and *patience,* Lucille,
but the pit bull is six bricks short of a full load."

GEORGE BOOTH

"I've come for your fleas."

JOHN CALDWELL

"Everyone should have, at least in spirit,
an enthusiastic dog."

LIZA DONNELLY

DAVID PASCAL

VAHAN SHIRVANIAN

"He doesn't bite, but there are zillions of germs
on his tongue."

REX MAY (BALOO)

"Who would've dreamed he'd be this jealous over a new baby?"

WILLIAM MAUL

OLD DOG/ NEW TRICK

MICK STEVENS

"I had that nightmare again. The one where I'm walking
down the street stark naked."

ED FRASCINO

FELIPE GALINDO (FEGGO)

"Poor thing! He just seems to *know* that something terrible
is happening in Afghanistan!"

ED FISHER

TONY ROSA

". . . and yet, she did not think only of herself. She always
considered the wishes of others. No matter how depressed
she was, no matter how tired she was, if you threw
a stick and told her to 'fetch' . . ."

SIDNEY HARRIS

"He eats every five minutes on the fifth minute."

BORIS DRUCKER

CHARLES ADDAMS

LO LINKERT

OBEDIENCE SCHOOL

"Of course you don't notice any difference, sir—
I taught him to obey *me!*"

JARED LEE

"Cut that out!"

PHIL INTERLANDI

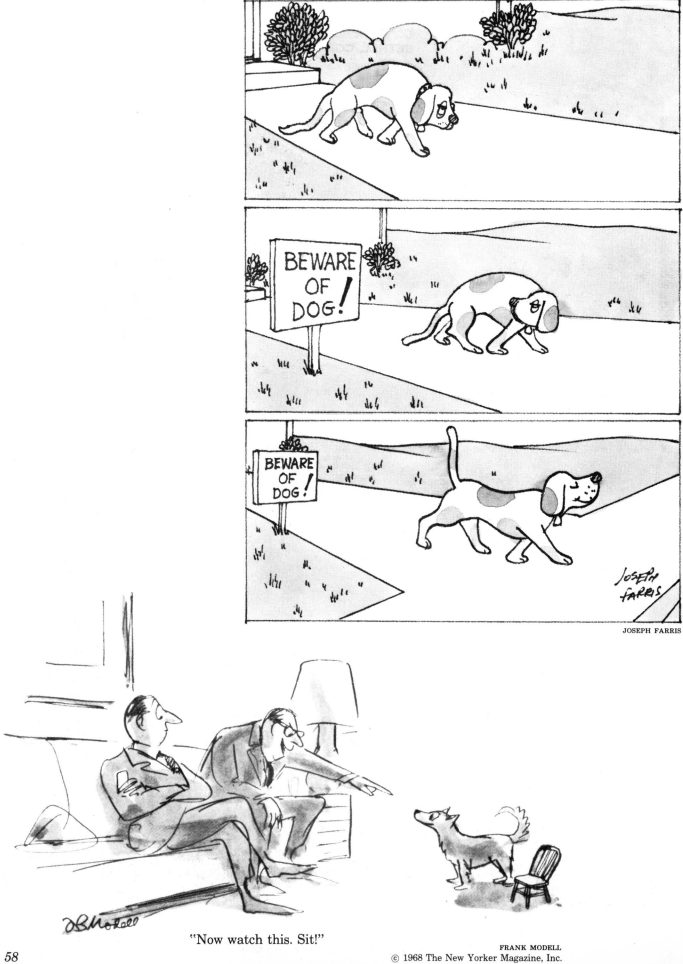

JOSEPH FARRIS

"Now watch this. Sit!"

FRANK MODELL
© 1968 The New Yorker Magazine, Inc.

MICHAEL CRAWFORD

"Yes, it's true. You were adopted."

HENRY MARTIN

"We're trying to teach him not to jump up on people."

LEO CULLUM

"So you have killed. Any qualms about it?"

TIM HAGGERTY

BERNARD SCHOENBAUM

 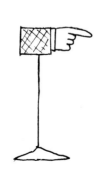   

S. GROSS

BRIAN SAVAGE
Reprinted courtesy *OMNI* magazine © 1981.

62

GEORGE BOOTH

"You're allergic to . . ."

SIDNEY HARRIS

"I'll prove it wasn't Tramp. . . . Here boy, here boy . . . !"

DONALD OREHEK

JACK ZIEGLER

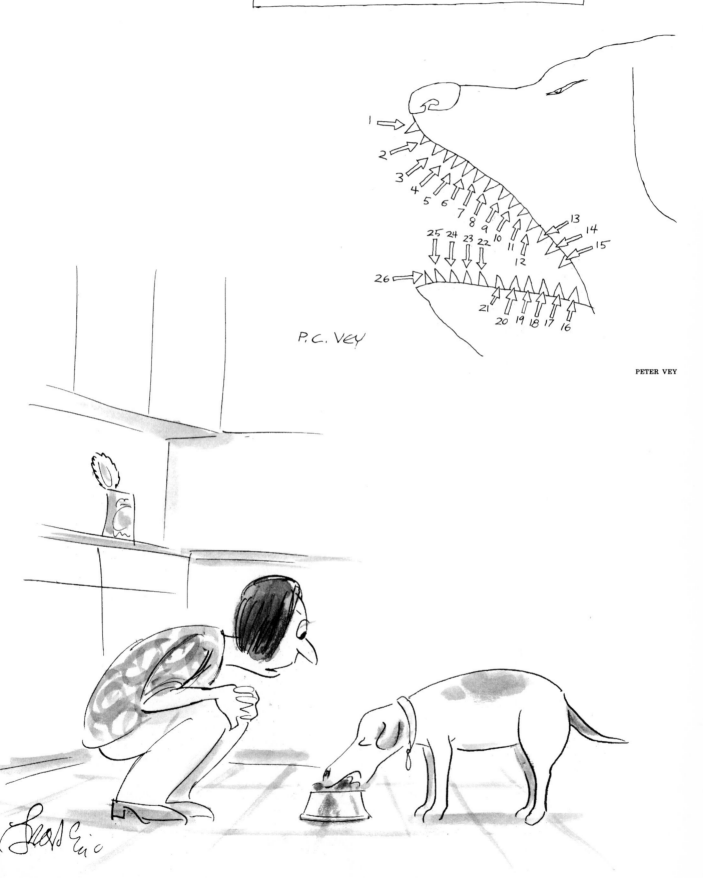

26 WARNING SIGNS OF THE DOG BITE

P.C. VEY

PETER VEY

"How do you like it when someone watches *you* eat?"

ED FRASCINO

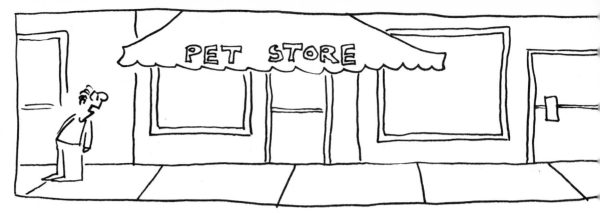

"Will you come on? I was kidding!"

"That happens to be *my* chair!"

MORT GERBERG

LIZA DONNELLY

U.S. POST OFFICE

VAHAN SHIRVANIAN

DR. PLAUT
VETERINARIAN

"I sure hope you can do that right. I'm tired of having to find
a new vet after every shot."

ORLANDO BUSINO

67

MORT GERBERG

"Now you know which one to push, Peppy. Push 'one.'"

BILL WOODMAN

DONALD OREHEK

JOHN JONIK

"Thank God we only do this once a month."

BUD GRACE

PETER PORGES

CATHARINE O'NEILL

"He's looking right at you, too. I hope you're proud of yourself
for saving eight cents on that brand."

"It doesn't just say 'dog'—it says 'hot dog'!"

AL ROSS

VAHAN SHIRVANIAN

"It's heavy panting. It must be for you."

MORT GERBERG

"These are his sunset years."

ROBERT WEBER

"Give me a call when he gets over that lisp."

JERRY MARCUS

Zack Brillard and Live-In Companion

ROBERT MANKOFF
© 1984 The New Yorker Magazine, Inc.

ARNIE LEVIN

"For heaven's sake, say 'please.'"

BERNARD SCHOENBAUM

"Go fetch."

TIM HAGGERTY

"Excuse me, Reverend. Your pup runneth over."

ANDY WYATT

"Valerie at Puppy Preen created the cut especially for her."

ED FRASCINO

BOOTH.
GEORGE BOOTH
© 1980 The New Yorker Magazine, Inc.

"... except ours had a shorter tail and slightly longer ears."

WILLIAM MAUL

"What about me? When do I get breakfast in bed?"

LEO CULLUM

DAVID JACOBSON

COMPLAINTS

S. GROSS

"He's very much involved with the moon."

BORIS DRUCKER
© 1980 The New Yorker Magazine, Inc.

BRIAN SAVAGE

ED ARNO

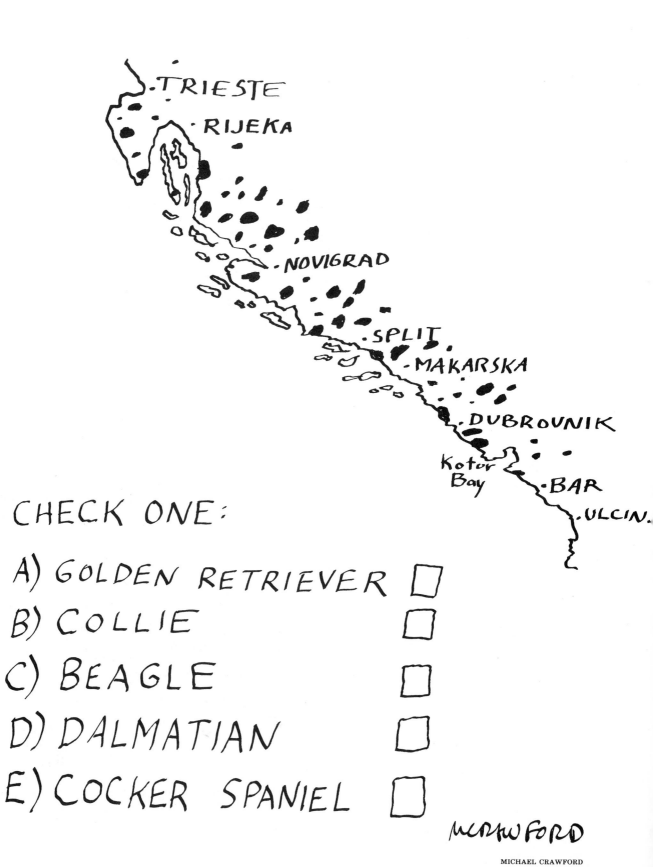

NAME THAT COAST!

CHECK ONE:

A) GOLDEN RETRIEVER ☐
B) COLLIE ☐
C) BEAGLE ☐
D) DALMATIAN ☐
E) COCKER SPANIEL ☐

MICHAEL CRAWFORD

86

"Good boy!"

ORLANDO BUSINO

JACK ZIEGLER

BILL WOODMAN

CALLAHAN

"Isn't it amazing how people look like their dogs!"

JOHN CALLAHAN

"Of course you can serve him. He's 3½. That's
way over 21 in human terms."

SIDNEY HARRIS

MORT GERBERG

CATHARINE O'NEILL

DAVID PASCAL

"Hot sidewalk."

RICHARD ORLIN

"Did I mention I have a dog?"

LIZA DONNELLY

"A four-letter word
meaning threads . . ."

". . . that cross the warp
in a woven fabric."

"Woof!"

BERNARD SCHOENBAUM

94

CHIPS' CUTENESS GRAPH

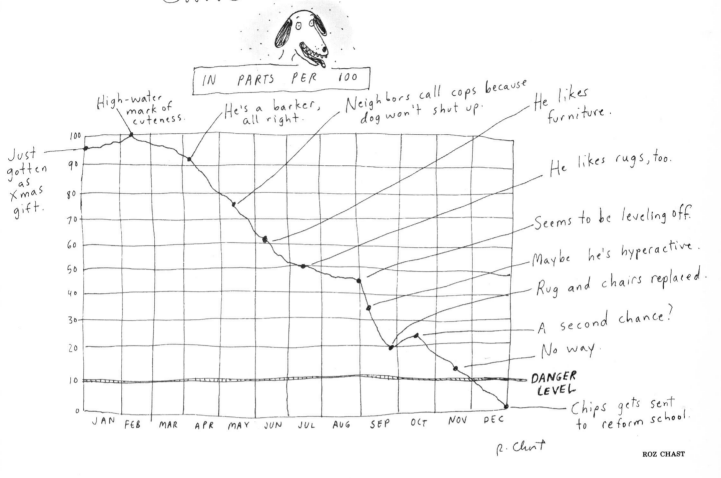

IN PARTS PER 100

Just gotten as Xmas gift.

High-water mark of cuteness.

He's a barker, all right.

Neighbors call cops because dog won't shut up.

He likes furniture.

He likes rugs, too.

Seems to be leveling off.

Maybe he's hyperactive.

Rug and chairs replaced.

A second chance?

No way.

DANGER LEVEL

Chips gets sent to reform school.

JAN FEB MAR APR MAY JUN JUL AUG SEP OCT NOV DEC

R. Chast

ROZ CHAST

"It has something to do with animal magnetism."

DAVID SIPRESS

SIPRESS

MORT GERBERG

"The late, great Snookie."

ED FRASCINO

"The management apologizes for serving the identical entree
on consecutive days and begs your understanding and indulgence."

WILLIAM MAUL

"He was chasing his tail and caught it."

DONALD OREHEK

"He's good at finding drugs, I grant you, but must he always give his opinion as to their quality?"

BRIAN SAVAGE

"Fifty dollars! He only cost two dollars new."

BUD GRACE

CLAES OLDENBURG'S DOG
AFTER A VISIT TO CHRISTO
JAVACHEFF'S STUDIO

MICK STEVENS

"It says, 'If found, please look in the newspaper's
Lost and Found column to see if we want him back.'"

SIDNEY HARRIS

"Spot."

VAHAN SHIRVANIAN

THE
RIGHT
TREE

Nurit

NURIT KARLIN

"Look, if I'm boring you, say so."

BOOTH '85

GEORGE BOOTH

FRANK MODELL

OK.... THIS WON'T TAKE LONG. WE'LL HAVE A PICTURE IN SECONDS. NOW HOLD IT...

CLICK!

CHUUUNGKALOOP!

LIZA DONNELLY

CALLAHAN

"So that's why they call them pit bulls!"

JOHN CALLAHAN

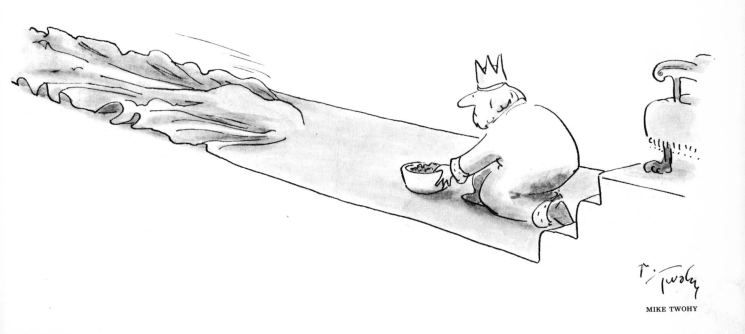

MIKE TWOHY

P. C. VEY

"Well, he certainly must have been a *good* dog!"

PETER VEY

"I should warn you—he's friendly enough when you pet him,
but don't stop."

ORLANDO BUSINO

BERNARD SCHOENBAUM

"Just because it's a doggie bag doesn't mean it's for you."

ANDY WYATT

"So you're the one who gave her to the ASPCA!"

TIM HAGGERTY

JERRY MARCUS

1.

2.

3.

4.

© BOOTH '85

GEORGE BOOTH

"... and another good thing about working here, they tend to promote
from within."

AARON BACALL

"Oh, for heaven's sake. Why don't you two kiss and make up?"

ED FRASCINO

MANKOF

ROBERT MANKO

ED FISHER

"Guess what! Mr. Corbett's going to be our lord and master."

FRANK MODELL

© 1969 The New Yorker Magazine, Inc.

CHARLES ADDAMS

CALDWELL

JOHN CALDWELL

1.

2.

3.

ARNIE LEVIN
© 1977 The New Yorker Magazine, Inc.

the
quick
brown
fox
jumps
over
the
lazy
+ dog
_____
abcdefghijklmnopqrstuvwxyz

JACK ZIEGLER

MICHAEL CRAWFORD

"Granted every boy should have a dog—but can't they all have the same one?"

SIDNEY HARRIS

"Let's see, I have Rex's pills, his medical record,
and his flea powder—yet, I can't help feeling
we've forgotten something."

ORLANDO BUSINO

"He certainly is not just *a* dog. He's *my* dog."

BERNARD SCHOENBAUM

"Try a couple of mouthfuls yourself, then he'll eat it."

DONALD OREHEK

"I knew it was a mistake to let him buy an Irish setter."

ORLANDO BUSINO

"I'll be right out, I'm taking a shower!"

JOHN CALDWELL

ALEX NOEL WATSON

BERNARD SCHOENBAUM

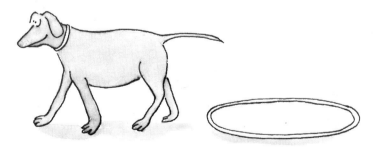

LEO CULLUM

SIPRESS

DAVID SIPRESS

"Here he is, Mr. Caruthers. Time to go home."

AL ROSS

© 1979 The New Yorker Magazine, Inc.

SIDNEY HARRIS

"I must apologize for Sophia. She hates goodbyes."

ED FRASCINO

"Do you mind if we browse?"

CHARLES SAUERS

"Why can't you walk your stinking dogs at night, Comrade Pavlov?"

BRIAN SAVAGE

"Look, Fufee, dear! A birthday wish to you from Dr. Cottinger
at the Bridgeview Small Animal Hospital."

HENRY MARTIN

"I thought you bird dogs were supposed to be so smart. Why, you can't even find the house I built for you!"

WILLIAM MAUL

TONY ROSA

BERNARD SCHOENBAUM
© 1982 The New Yorker Magazine, Inc.

"Don't feed him, Joe. That's as big
as I want him to get."

JOHN NORMENT

DAVID PASCAL

BOOTH.

GEORGE BOOTH

"Bootsie! I hope these aren't dog hairs in my hair of the dog again!"

JACK ZIEGLER

DONALD OREHEK

"Out, out, damned Spot!"

MORT GERBERG

"When you have four fat St. Bernards in the truck, you have to take it easy around corners!"

ORLANDO BUSINO

VAHAN SHIRVANIAN

STUART LEEDS

"Try not to eat him, all right?"

BILL WOODMAN

"Boooo Woooo."

ANDY WYATT

BOOTH

GEORGE BOOTH

JOHN CALDWELL

"It's an ideal relationship. He does everything I tell him."

ED FRASCINO

1.

2.

3.

4.

BERNARD SCHOENBAUM

"I don't know if Rusty can sleep over. Which one *is* Rusty?"

SIDNEY HARRIS

"That's not funny!"

ED FISHER

"I knew we shouldn't have stayed for that second rubber
of bridge. He's been crying."

ED FRASCINO

FRANK MODELL

"I need a loan for his doghouse."

ORLANDO BUSINO

"That pooch really put up a tough battle
when I put him out last night, honey!"

DONALD OREHEK

NURIT KARLIN

BOOTH

GEORGE BOOTH

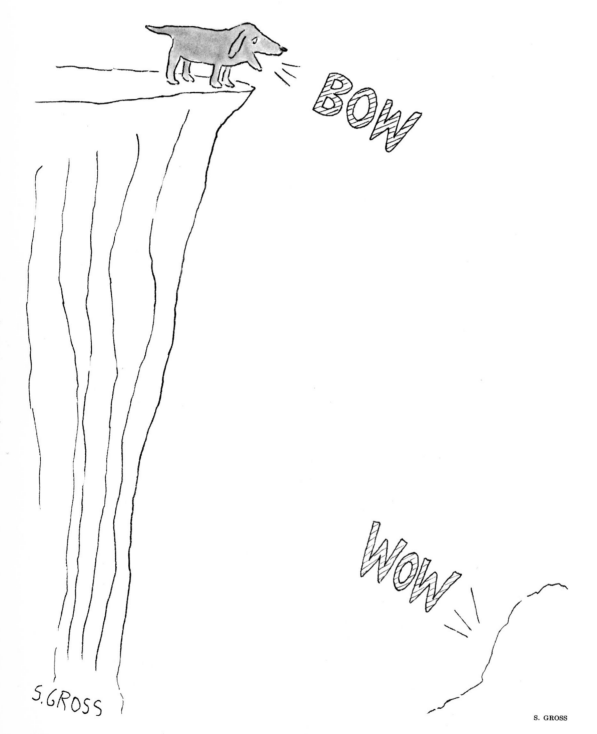

S. GROSS

THESE PREMISES PROTECTED BY TRAINED GUARD DOGS

MORT GERBERG

"Don't sit in the dark. Turn the TV on for the dog."

BORIS DRUCKER

① ② ③ ④

LEE LORENZ
© 1983 The New Yorker Magazine, Inc.

"Levez-vous tout de suite!"

BERNARD SCHOENBAUM

PHIL INTERLANDI

BERNARD SCHOENBAUM

GAHAN WILSON

"I choose all her friends."

ED FRASCINO

"Training dogs to protest. That's the lowest of the low!"

AL ROSS

SIDNEY HARRIS

"Aha! So that's how my books get dog-eared."

ORLANDO BUSINO

"Poor Fifi hasn't been the same since the veterinarian put the brain of his hunchbacked assistant into her skull!"

GAHAN WILSON

"Offhand I'd say the guarantee on his flea collar is about to expire."

WILLIAM MAUL

SERGIO ARAGONES

1

2

3

4

5

JACOBSON

DAVID JACOBSON

152

CALLAHAN

"Looks like rain—better put on Chester's booties."

JOHN CALLAHAN

"Ever since you've learned to talk, all we've done is argue."

HENRY MARTIN

"Mr. Bellfort, your dog to see you."

ED FRASCINO

HOW TO DRAW A DOG

STEP 1. ALWAYS DRAW THE TAIL FIRST. IT'S THE EASIEST PART AND WILL GET YOU OFF TO A GOOD START.

STEP 2. NOW ADD THE PAWS. REMEMBER, THE DOG IS A QUADRUPED, SO YOU'LL NEED FOUR OF THEM.

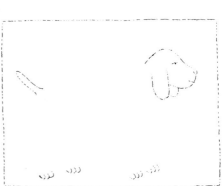

STEP 3. NEXT IS THE HEAD WHICH IS BASICALLY AN OVAL WITH EARS. AND THERE YOU HAVE IT, EXCEPTING THE BODY AND THE REST OF THE LEGS WHICH ARE OPTIONAL

MANKOFF

ROBERT MANKOFF

DONNELLY

LIZA DONNELLY

BUSINO

ORLANDO BUSINO

"After you've stretched your awareness you might split open a can of dog food."

GEORGE BOOTH

"Why don't you live your life and let me live mine?"

BERNARD SCHOENBAUM

"Look, Champ. I've brought you someone to help with the slippers!"

CATHARINE O'NEILL

3.

2.

1.

4.

VAHAN SHIRVANIAN

"She's the glue that holds this family together!"

BRIAN SAVAGE

"I had a jar of mint jelly in my rucksack and now it's gone.
Do you want to talk about it?"

TIM HAGGERTY

DOG TIRED

HENRY MARTIN

BERNARD SCHOENBAUM

"No swimming! He just ate."

ED FRASCINO

"I made a complete sweater from Goo-Goo and I think
Cleopatra will make a real pretty scarf."

ANDY WYATT

BILL WOODMAN

THOMAS CHENEY

"Speak."

"Whoever he brings it back to gets custody."

MIKE TWOHY

"Just remember the vet said he's going through mid-life crisis."

ED FRASCINO

"You *stay!* That's the trouble with all you poodles—always
coming out of the dryer too soon!"

MORT GERBERG

"Heel!"

S. GROSS

S. GROSS

BEWARE OF THE ~~DOG~~ SNAKE

CALDWELL

JOHN CALDWELL

"Let her go, Irene. They've all got references."

BUD GRACE

"Okay, Pepper, walk one more block then turn around and come home."

ORLANDO BUSINO

BERNARD SCHOENBAUM

"Don't tell me you have bad news, too."

FRANK MODELL
© 1978 The New Yorker Magazine, Inc.

FELIPE GALINDO (FEGGO)

"Mine are twins, too!"

BARNEY TOBEY

"You're certainly not the dog I thought you were."

ED FRASCINO

P.C. VEY

PETER VEY

"Neither of us are Slaytons, but Orange is descended
from their original setter."

BORIS DRUCKER

BERNARD SCHOENBAUM

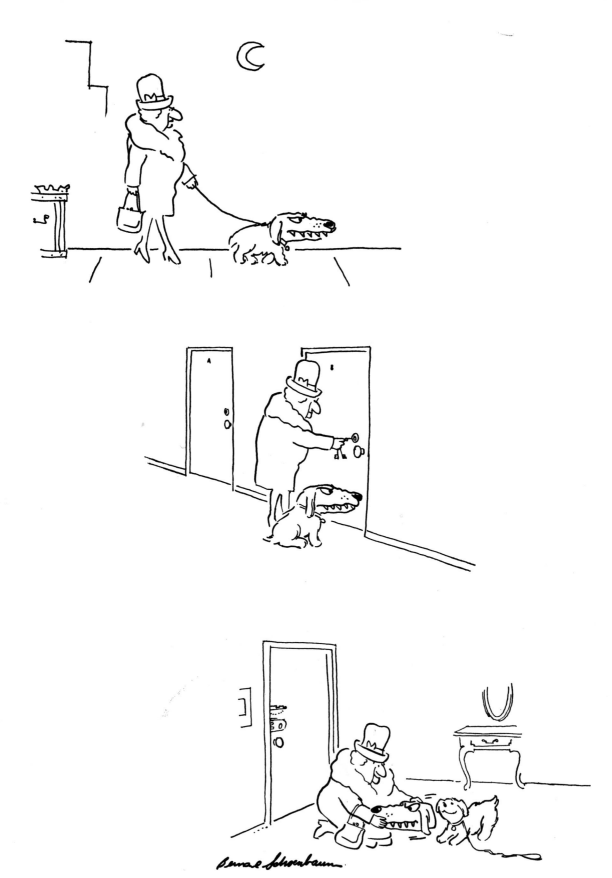

BERNARD SCHOENBAUM
© 1975 The New Yorker Magazine, Inc.

"It's not your fault, madam . . . he simply doesn't respond to petting."

THOMAS CHENEY

"So that's why his nose is always so cold."

ORLANDO BUSINO

SIDNEY HARRIS

JACK ZIEGLER

GEORGE BOOTH

"Go on up. I want to speak to Rubin privately."

ED FRASCINO

MIKE TWOHY

"This is Andy—and don't be concerned. He's only vicious
to strangers with their clothes on."

MORT GERBERG

WALK
YOUR
DOG

ARNIE LEVIN

FELIPE GALINDO (FEGGO)

"Just look at what you've become!"

BERNARD SCHOENBAUM

"Oh Tippy. Tippy, Tippy, Tippy! If only you didn't cook
with water from the toilet."

TIM HAGGERTY

LEO CULLUM

BUD GRACE

JOSEPH FARRIS

184

"We've been practicing all afternoon. . . . Act like
you're going to attack me. . . ."

DONALD OREHEK

"Lucky!"

ED FRASCINO

"How can you say we have nothing after all these years? I have you,
you have me, and we have a nice dog named Spotty."

"His license is here somewhere."

ORLANDO BUSINO

CHARLES ADDAMS

FELIPE GALINDO (FEGGO)

"He's a loner just like you."

BARNEY TOBEY

"You can still cut it, Frank, but Prince is too old
to be walking on his hind legs."

BORIS DRUCKER

"Will you stop scolding that poor animal? Can't you see he's sorry?"

"Time stands still for you."

ED FRASCINO

". . . and *this* goes beyond range of the human ear."

MORT GERBERG

BILL WOODMAN

Future Pup

MICK STEVENS

"This preparation will eliminate fleas, this one ticks,
this one various other vermin and considerable fungi,
and this one will eliminate the dog itself."

GAHAN WILSON

LOU MYERS

"I had a feeling those dogs were getting too damned smart."

"What do you think of that, Buster? The stupid cowboy
is talking to his horse."

MEL YAUK

JOHN JONIK

"That does it! Tomorrow he gets a haircut!"

WILLIAM MAUL

BERNARD SCHOENBAUM

INDEX

Addams, Charles, 30, 55, 114, 175, 187
Aragones, Sergio, 151
Arno, Ed, 85
Bacall, Aaron, 24, 111
Baloo (Rex May), 50
Barsotti, Charles, 32
Booth, George, 14, 47, 62, 80, 102, 110, 129, 134, 142, 156, 178
Brown, M. K., 37
Busino, Orlando, 20, 36, 67, 87, 106, 117, 120, 131, 140, 149, 155, 167, 176, 186
Caldwell, John, 23, 48, 114, 120, 135, 166
Callahan, John, 46, 90, 105, 153
Chast, Roz, 95
Cheney, Thomas, 37, 107, 163, 176, 198
Crawford, Michael, 59, 86, 116
Cullum, Leo, 9, 60, 82, 99, 122, 182
Donnelly, Liza, 3, 12, 48, 66, 93, 104, 155
Drucker, Boris, 24, 54, 84, 143, 173, 186, 190
Farris, Joseph, 58, 184
Feggo (Felipe Galindo), 52, 169, 181, 188
Fisher, Ed, 2, 13, 53, 113, 138
Frascino, Ed, 5, 18, 28, 51, 65, 79, 96, 112, 124, 135, 139, 147, 154, 161, 165, 172, 179, 185, 191, 192
Galindo, Felipe (Feggo), 52, 169, 181, 188
Gerberg, Mort, 19, 20, 66, 68, 75, 91, 96, 131, 143, 165, 180, 192
Grace, Bud, 41, 70, 100, 167, 183
Gross, S., 22, 61, 83, 142, 166
Haggerty, Tim, 8, 21, 60, 78, 109, 160, 182
Harris, Sidney, 23, 54, 63, 90, 101, 117, 124, 137, 148, 177
Hunt, Stan, 33
Interlandi, Phil, 57, 145
Jacobson, David, 43, 83, 152
Jonik, John, 70, 196
Karlin, Nurit, 21, 103, 141
Lee, Jared, 4, 57
Leeds, Stuart, 133
Levin, Arnie, 33, 45, 77, 115, 170, 180

Linkert, Lo, 56
Lorenz, Lee, 4, 45, 144, 164
Mankoff, Robert, 76, 112, 154
Marcus, Jerry, 5, 29, 76, 109
Martin, Henry, 59, 126, 153, 160
Maul, William, 2, 15, 50, 81, 97, 127, 150, 196
May, Rex (Baloo), 50
Miller, W., 68
Mirachi, Joe, 10, 195
Modell, Frank, 3, 6, 31, 42, 58, 73, 82, 103, 113, 139, 149, 151, 168, 190
Myers, Lou, 194
Norment, John, 129
O'Neill, Catharine, 19, 72, 92, 157
Orehek, Donald, 6, 31, 46, 63, 69, 97, 119, 130, 140, 185
Orlin, Richard, 42, 93
Pascal, David, 48, 92, 128
Porges, Peter, 71
Rosa, Tony, 53, 127
Ross, Al, 73, 123, 148
Sauers, Charles, 27, 125
Savage, Brian, 32, 62, 84, 98, 126, 159
Saxon, Charles, 1, 118
Schoenbaum, Bernard, 7, 26, 61, 77, 94, 108, 119, 121, 128, 136, 145, 146, 157, 161, 168, 173, 174, 181, 191, 197
Shirvanian, Vahan, 10, 25, 49, 67, 74, 102, 132, 158
Sipress, David, 28, 44, 95, 123
Steiner, Peter, 8, 18
Stevens, Mick, 51, 101, 193
Tobey, Barney, 17, 81, 171, 189
Twohy, Mike, 35, 105, 164, 179
Vey, Peter, 13, 65, 106, 172
Watson, Alex Noel, 121
Weber, Robert, 25, 75
Wilson, Gahan, 27, 147, 150, 194
Woodman, Bill, 11, 16, 38, 69, 88, 133, 162, 193
Wyatt, Andy, 11, 34, 79, 108, 134, 162
Yauk, Mel, 99, 195
Ziegler, Jack, 14, 34, 64, 87, 115, 130, 177